We All Have Those Days

Brookie Cowles

To all the Loves in my life:
You inspire my greatest work.

Table of Contents:

By Owen

Scream scream
All night long
Til the sun
Comes along.
Will you please
Be my song?
     I will sing for you

6/26/15

By Jack

If I say it louder
Does it mean I care more?
I LIKE TRAINS! I LIKE TRAINS!
Oh, by the way, I'm four.

6/26/15

Happy Birthday Lady Bug

Can walk
Can't skip
Can sing
Can't read
Can undress
Can't dress
Can eat
Can't cook
Can play
Can't ride
Can climb
Can't repel
Can snuggle
Can hug
Can Kiss
So big yet so small. I love how you've grown,
but I'm sad all the same. One of life's
dilemmas.

Happiness Comes to Those Who Want It

Books on top of beds
        Books underneath beds
               Books on Shelves
Books on floors
       Books in the kitchen
Books near the bath
            Books in my closet
Books in my hands

Peace is a shower after a long day.
Peace is a cup of hot chocolate.
Peace is a book in your hand and rain on your window.
Peace is children playing together.
Peace is singing a baby to sleep.
Peace is a song on the radio that speaks to your heart.
Peace is a hug after time away.
Peace is a crackling fireplace.
Peace is sitting with someone you love on a bench under an old oak tree.
Peace is.

There was a town filled with happiness.
All of the people felt only gladness.
One day they took all of their sorrows
to the old woman who promised tomorrow's
filled with laughter and joy and smiles,
nothing to cry over, no worries for miles.

The people were joyful, filled with content,
"No worries or cares, she's heaven sent."
So, they went about the day with a skip and a
hop.
They did only happy things and never forgot
the old woman who carried all of their sorrow
and promised joy for every tomorrow.

Generations passed, the old woman was there,
carrying each burden, taking each care.
This group of people never felt sad.
They only felt what was supposed to be glad.
But without sorrow to balance it out,
They never found anything to be happy about.

They soon grew bored, and fell into depression.
They needed something to give them expression.
One day the old woman filled a bucket with
stress,
poured it into the streets and made a big mess.
Confused and worried, they didn't know what to
do.
They got angry and bitter and then they blamed
you.

*****

But some realized what the old woman had done.
They scooped up the stress and mixed it with fun.
They worked hard to keep their buckets from spilling,
and tried each day to add real joy to the filling.
They found that their joy was greater than before,
because, with sorrow, it meant much more.

Some people read books for adventure
Some for the world
Some for the magic
Some for the lesson.
Of course, those are all good,
but I read for the romance.
The spark between two people,
that drive, their need for each other.
I need the hope for happiness,
that despite the odds,
they can be together
Forever.
Because they are made for each other,
the strength to their weakness,
the second half of their soul,
all that cliché stuff.
Because that's what romance is.
And that makes me happy.
And that's why I read books.

Halloween night brings magic and fun
Candy and costumes for everyone
But you'd better beware
And you'd better watch out
Because witches and black cats linger about

The witches come out leaving their forts
They wear black hats to hide all their warts
They fly on their brooms
Through all the dark streets
Casting a spell on all that they meet

Black cats come out and keep to the dark
They sit in quiet and watch their mark
Which is you, of course
They're silent and mean
And hoping to scare you and cause you to scream

The Jack-O-Lanterns are the spies
For witches to watch you through pumpkin eyes
They sit at each door
And then report back
About all of the costumes and scary masks

So when you go out on Halloween night
Be sure to look to your left and right
For witches and cats
And Jack-O-Lanterns too
They will catch you and scare you and then shout BOO!

Snow falling
Bells jingling
Lights twinkling
It's Christmastime

Singers caroling
Cocoa steaming
Present shopping
It's Christmastime

Children dreaming
Snowmen building
Stars gleaming
It's Christmastime

Together sitting
Fires crackling
Hearts brimming
It's Christmastime

You say you don't
but you really do.
Nerves rack your body
through and through.
This whole thing
is just so new,
but secretly you're excited,
it's true.

Randomness Makes the World Go Round

Distance

I don't really run
I just say I do because
It makes me seem cool

Nyquil

I bring you sleep
like never before,
You will be begging
for more and more,
But if you wake
before my will,
I promise hangovers,
I am Nyquil

Haiku

No writing today.
A poem adds word count, right?
Writing finished? Check.

Too sleepy to write
A haiku will have to count
As my Poem a Day

I am so tired
I can no longer function
Now sleep must ensue.

Good night, moon,
Good night stars.
Good night world,
Good night hearts.

Prepared

Practice = Prepared

Consistent practice = Prepared

Determined, consistent practice= Prepared

Unfalteringly determined, consistent practice = Prepared

Tenacious, unfalteringly determined, consistent practice = Prepared

Resolutely tenacious, unfalteringly determined, consistent practice = Prepared

Resolutely tenacious resolve to succeed, unfalteringly determined to be the best, consistent practice, working for hours upon hours, with sweat dripping down and blood pooling; a paragon, a model, a hero in your own right refusing to quit = Perfection

Wait, I mean Prepared

Experience

There's something about experience
It's really something funny
You think you are more
Than the rich or the poor
Even without lots of money

But inexperience itself
Sings its own sort of tale
Of naïveté
And dumb things you say
Needing experience without fail

The moral left to learn
About the two just the same
One can be fixed
By adding one to the mix
Balance is the name of the game

How To Prepare for High School

Long hair
  preferably blonde
    but I suppose a very dark brown works, too
Perfect eye brows
  expensive ones that you pay to have maintained
Clear skin
  not a blemish
Pouty lips
  the really pouty kind
      because constant duck lips are so hot
Size 2 body
  toned, not flabby, thin, but not anorexic.
    Seriously, there is an equation to this
Tanned, of course
  who wants to see your white legs?
    Remember when white skin was preferred?
     HAHAHAHAHAHA
Shaved legs
  obviously
    or you might as well skip the tan because you'll be in
pants FOREVER
      And pants...no
Manicured hands and feet
  with a sparkly color
  or a bold solid, a statement color
Designer handbag
  the more expensive the better.
    They can tell when it's a knock-off. Don't go there.
Shoes
  do NOT think about wearing those Chuck Taylors.
    Wear a name brand sandal that you can't actually
wear to the beach   *****

Clothes are an entirely different story
   just pick something that is dry clean only
      and make sure Life doesn't touch it
         or you might just be laughed at for having a stain
right on the front
Smile
   no one wants to be friends with a pouter
      and you are clearly pouting if there is no smile on your
face
Good luck! Enjoy your day.
   Don't stress, you'll do great.
      It's not really that scary. It's only High School.

Of Princes and Princesses

Cinderella went to the ball,
She was fairest of them all.
She danced in sparkling crystal shoes,
As the sky darkened to blue.

When midnight struck, she ran away
To hide the truth she wore each day.
She would hide in her ashes and soot,
And cherish the glass worn on her foot.

But what if, instead, she chose to stay?
What would the startled prince have to say
When the beautiful girl turned to grime?
I doubt he'd whisper, "You are mine."

But, since she fled the Prince's arms
She left behind her winning charms.
Therefore, in love he searched and wandered.
Absence makes the heart grow fonder.

A Daddy is a daughter's Prince Charming,
    the man she wants to marry.
As she grows, a Daddy becomes
    the man she runs to when she's scared,
    when she wants to dance,
    when she's proud.
A Daddy is the man from whom she learns
    the kind of man she wants to love forever.
That's when a Daddy
    Becomes a Dad.

A daughter is a daddy's princess,
    the second (behind her mother) to own his
heart,
    the girl he spoils, and loves, and cherishes,
    because of her preciousness.
As she grows, a daughter becomes
    someone a Daddy wants to protect.
No little boy will be good enough
    for the girl who makes his heart swell.
A daughter is a Daddy's little girl
    even when she's old.
And somewhere along the line this Daddy
        Becomes a Dad.

Her name is Lucy,
Lucy by the Sea.
She has hopes and dreams,
And places to be.
Lucy by the sea.

She wanted to see Paris
And also Peru.
She wanted to see Rome,
And India too.
Lucy by the sea

She wanted to go abroad
To see elephants and things.
She wanted to see palaces
And Queens and Kings.
Lucy by the sea.

She wanted to study philosophy,
Languages, arts, and more
She wanted to paint the birds
That ate along the shore.
Lucy by the Sea.

****

She wanted to feel love,
The magic of first kiss,
She wanted to capture a heart,
Oh, the things she would miss.
Lucy by the Sea.

The smell of fresh bread,
The morning sun,
The touch of a flower,
The feel of a run.
The words in a book,
The music around,
The feel of the dew,
The grass on the ground.

But it's time to say goodbye
It's the way things must be.
It's spreading throughout her,
And killing her body.
Lucy by the Sea.

We meet and my heart stops.
You are the most handsome man
I have ever seen,
Golden hair and blue eyes,
Tall and fit,
And...sneering at me?
Why?
What did I do to deserve that?
My toe catches on the ground
And I stumble
Unsure how to proceed.
I decide on Beauty,
On grace,
So, I smile politely
And shake your hand
But you refuse.
You cannot be expected to
Touch someone like me.
Your laugh
And your sneer
Make you ugly.
You are nothing more
Than a Beast.

Deep in the ocean,
under the sea,
glides a mermaid,
merrily.

She sings to the fish,
talks with the birds.
A voice of angels,
have you heard?

With hair that burns red,
emerald eyes,
skin made of cream,
many despise.

No wonder the witch-
envious, true-
wanted her voice,
and beauty too.

There was a girl
Who was quite content,
But she never smiled
No one knew what it meant.

All day long she would hear
Smile bigger than that!
What is wrong with you?
Why are you so sad?

That straight lined smile
Isn't good enough
It is your teeth
We want to see more of

Show your teeth
Your dimples too
Everyone wants
To see the real you!

She thought in wonder
I am being me.
I'm smiling my best,
Why can't they see?

If something is wrong
With my straight smile,
Has something been wrong
With me all this while?

*****

Can I be enough
The way that I am,
Or must I change me
To fit in their plan?

Always doubting herself
She went through her life,
Afraid that her smile
Would cause more strife.

But no one knew that
While she sat content
Her eyes smiled for her
They sparkled instead

She enjoyed watching
The world go by.
She loved the sunshine
Was afraid of the night.

She was just like you
And just like me too.
Her smile was beautiful
Through and through.

The Unassuming Princess
She was a girl
with eyes of blue,
ringleted hair
of golden hue.

She wanted adventure
more than anyone.
She put on her boots
and looked for some fun.

She trained with a witch,
learned how to use spells,
dined with three bears,
bested a dragon as well.

Adventure surrounded
full of pleasure and delight.
Something new at each corner
every day and night.

Until one day when
the King summoned her.
She went to the castle
nervous, unsure.

But the King didn't greet her,
it was the Prince instead
who kissed her fingers,
knelt down, and said:

"Fair maiden
with eyes of blue
rumors have spread
and I know about you.   *****

You live for adventure,
the wide outdoors,
but I wonder if you
are up for one more?

Marry me,
Beautiful one,
I promise our life
will be filled with fun.

We'll see the world
inside and out.
We'll visit places
you only hear about.

But do it with me
standing at your side,
your spirit is enchanting,
please be my bride?"

She stared for a moment.
Could this be true?
Could someone love
her adventurousness too?

"Of course dear Prince,
with chocolate colored hair,
let's take an adventure
everywhere.

Let's see the land
and the ocean blue.
I want to adventure
with someone like you"   *****

Soon they were married,
an adventure of it's own,
they kissed in front of thousands
awaiting their love to be shown

Then they departed,
the Prince with brown hair
keeping her blue eyes
safe in his care.

Happily ever after
is sure to ensue
for the prince and his maiden
and their adventurousness too.

Her name means Beauty
And she is Beauty entirely
Inside and out
When he came along
Beastly and growling
All limbs and snout
She loved him
Without a doubt

Nature

Pure white
And alone
Surrounded by green
And water droplets
Flower sits among the leaves
Light against the dark

My Doodle Poem

Sometimes I like to doodle
I draw flowers and clouds and trees
With a pen in my hand
  or a finger in sand,
I loop and I swirl freely.

Little blossoms
perched on a branch,
bristling in the wind,
reaching for the sun.
Soon you will be leaves
and fruit to eat,
but for now, you are beautiful.

Advent Calendar Sky

Grey clouds bunch together
forming envelope fluffs
waiting to be opened
and show their surprise
in my advent calendar sky

The first is lightning
with thunder close behind
promising raindrops
from their pouch
in my advent calendar sky

Next holds a downpour
the kind that floods the streets
and bathes the world
bringing new life from high
in my advent calendar sky

The last envelope waits
for the others to open
its gift is the rainbow
the beauty ending the storm
in my advent calendar sky

When you wake up to cold
crisp morning air
the leaves look a shade darker
geese fly overhead
and you know
It's Fall

The calendar might not confirm
but that doesn't matter
you pull out sweaters
boots and scarves
because you know
It's Fall

You're ready for fireplaces
knit blankets and socks
you open windows
and cherish the cool air
you know
It's Fall

Tall and unyielding
Steady and firm
Brown and green
Red and purple
Yellow and pink
Orange too
Beautiful trees

White clouds float
     In a boat
          Of blue sky

Wispy Shreds
     Fluffy beds
          Dance and fly

Block the sun
     Windy run
          They glide by

The thing that I hate about winter,
The thing that winter's about,
Is the snow all around
Covering the ground
Freezing me inside and out

But snow can be lovely sometimes
Watching from inside is best,
Under the heater
Becoming a reader,
With blankets and chocolate and rest.

Nature

Rain swells and billows.
The world, a liquid blanket
creating new life.

Hot Chocolate on a Summer Morning

Sunrise and puffy clouds
Not a word is said aloud
Birds chatter and trees talk
Steaming cup while I walk
Hot chocolate on a summer morning

Marshmallows disintegrate
Foam starts to congregate
Burning sip in my mouth
First I spit, then I shout
Hot chocolate on a summer morning

Birds scatter at the sound
People start to move around
Pour milk into the mug
flick away another bug
Hot chocolate on a summer morning

Morning now full of noise
Breakfast, laughter, and some toys
Time of solace in the past
Knowing it would never last
Hot chocolate on a summer morning

In a world
full of
people, how
can I feel so
alone?

I waited for
You to throw
Open the door
Desperately
Begging
For one more

Another kiss
Before
Goodnight
A sending off
And then
Sleep tight

But the door
Remained closed
And still locked
I fell asleep
Completely
Shocked

Train Station

I lost you today.
You walked away
And I didn't run after.

I stood on the platform
Wondering
What I wanted more,

A new life?
Or you?

The doors closed.
I guess I made my choice.
I didn't even cry.

A Poem for Midnight

I'm drowning
I'm gasping for air
But it's not there,
You're not here
And I'm still drowning

You left without goodbye.
What was I to think?
That all was fine?
You'd be right back?
Emotions filled to the brink.

I called out your name
I begged you to stay
afraid to let go
afraid of alone.
You turned and went on your way.

I broke down in sobs
I cried hours longer
it did me no good
you never came home
but my tears made me stronger

The whisper of words left unspoken
float around me.
I feel a graze as each passes by
and I wonder
Can this be fixed?

An Open Position

I had one once.
A friend.
We were sisters at heart,
Never apart.
I had one once,
A friend.

Looking for you
My friend.
You have gone away now,
But I need you.
Looking for you,
My friend.

A position
To fill
Kind, and true, and loyal,
Can that be you?
A position
To fill.

Midnight Musings

Sometimes I feel like I'm five
I just can't get along
I try, I really do
But it comes out all wrong

Why can't we all be friends?
Why can't we just be kind?
We cut each other down
Without a care in mind.

What if we looked at intent?
What would we see on the heart?
Would we see malice
Or see love to impart?

Grown ups think they know all,
Find fault and blame ensues.
But they cannot forgive
Anything that you do.

Maybe it's best to be five.
It's easy to forget,
Say sorry, and smile,
Be forever friends yet.

Some days are harder than others
when I think back to
how it used to be
I feel like I failed you,
I feel like I hardly know you.
I think back and my heart pains
    to see your sweet innocent smile
    to see the light of joy in your eyes
I know life didn't steal that from you,
    You did that on your own.
But maybe life can steal
the pain my heart feels
each time I look at you

Writers Block

I want to write something
I really do
But nothing is coming to mind
Except you

I miss you baby
It's true
Come back home now
Please do

#2

Today is a hard day
I woke up thinking about you
    about how it used to be
    about your smile
    about your eyes
        They were always your best trait
        -Eyes are the windows to the soul-
But there is no light there,
no joy.
It has been replaced with artificial happiness
And my heart breaks,
split at the seams,
And tears roll down my face.
I hope time will heal
this loss I feel,
    Each time I see your face.
But the pain is what helps
me remember
How much I love you.

You'd think I'd go to sleep early
Because I see you when my eyes are closed
Instead, I'm awake
Oh for heavens sake!
If I'm lucky, I'll finally doze.

I take a gasping breath.
It's an involuntary reaction
To my body's need for oxygen,
But it doesn't solve my problem,
You're still not here.
So, I go on holding my breath
Til you come home.

I know that you're leaving
I can feel it
Time is running out
I can't stop it
Please just stay
Don't go away
I can't live without you

All that's left is memory
And I hate it
Of you and me together
I don't want it
Too much I miss
And that last kiss
How could you walk away?

Remember that time we went swimming
In that pond with the rope swing?
Remember that time at the market
When we tasted everything?
Remember when you loved me, and I called you
mine?
Remember, remember, remember that time...

Now I'm alone every day
And I need you
You've moved on, but I can't
I loved you
I know you're gone
I need to move on
The memories won't leave me alone.

I listen to the Silence
That comes from a
Sleeping house

It's a living Silence
Breathing, haunting
Keeping me company

A silence I hear
And feel wrapped around me
A blanket in the cold

I see what you're trying to do,
You're at it again.
How can you live life this way?
You have no sense of what is true.

Does manipulating get what you want?
You do it so often; it's all you know.
But for some reason we all fall for it,
You mess with our minds with out any thought.

But I don't have to take this,
What would I lose?
I have my own life now,
There's nothing about you to miss.

I know that's harsh of me to say,
But how much do I really know you?
Has it been a sham the entire time?
I don't like who you are today.

An Invisible Friend

I wanted to share today.
It was a special day after all.
A birthday!
I wanted to share today with you.

But you weren't around today.
You weren't there when I called
No answer!
You weren't around today.

I started to feel alone.
I wondered where you had gone.
My friend,
I started to feel alone

My best friend is a monster.
He tags along to wherever I go.
He talks to me throughout the day
And makes sure I know his opinion
About everything.
I can't see him,
But I know he's there
Making sure my decisions are rational
And well researched.
I never go wrong when I listen to him
Because I never do anything.
He keeps me in line.
His name is Fear.

Silence

There is a loneliness in Silence
Sometimes you don't know it's there
until you feel it so overwhelmingly
present
a need to open your mouth and speak
to know your words will be heard
by more than your mind
But Silence doesn't comfort
Silence doesn't respond
You are alone.

You know that feeling
like everything is going
fine
but you can't shake
the rock in your gut
or the claws on your heart
and you wonder
Why?
What am I missing?
Why am I hyperventilating
dreading the next second
when everything is
fine?

I am afraid
Of driving in snow
Of talking to people
Of saying the wrong thing
Of tripping in heels
Of wasting time
Of sun burning
Of bees
Of trying new food
Of being different
I am afraid
Of life

Panophobia

Claustrophobia, Astraphobia, Cynophobia,

Agoraphobia, Ophidiophobia, Arachnophobia,
Mysophobia,

Carcinophobia, Thanatophobia, Glossophonbia,

Atychiphobia, Trypanophobia, Xenophobia,
Metathesiophobia,

Nyctophobia, Entomophobia, Galeophobia

Panophobia

Alone
sole, isolated, abandoned,
unaccompanied, deserted, stag,
forsaken, solitary, individual,
alone

She stared at the sky
threatening to rain
and said
I know how you feel.
Except, you're allowed to cry
and I'm not.
They'll tell me to be brave,
but I just can't.
I want to be a cloud
and burst into rain when
I feel heavy,
and answer to no one.

Instead, she gritted her teeth
breathed in her rain
and continued her walk.

I should keep my mouth closed.
Then no one can be offended.
If words aren't said,
There's nothing for which to apologize.
Yet, I did apologize.

How can some people act like they don't care
When I bathe in worry, and regret?
How can they push everything out
When I internalize each word?
Why do I internalize?

It's better to keep quiet
I'll keep my mouth shut.
I won't be the problem
I won't cause regret.

It's better this way.

Happily Ever Afters are Food for the Soul

I wish for happily ever after
I wish for love in our next chapter
I wish for what we've always had
With you by me, I'm always glad

I want to write you a Love Poem

I want to write you a love poem
I want to show you my heart
I want you to understand
That I never wish to part

I want to write you a love song
I want there to be violins
I want you to hear the melody
That I have within

I want to write you a love story
I want it to be filled with laughter
I want us to always live
Happily Ever After

We walk holding hands
Walking with no demands
On time, just you and me
Effortlessly free.

#momlife

Woke up early this morning
No one else moved
The sun woke up with me
Spreading a golden hue.

I ran through my To-Do list
I planned the best route
To go about my errands
Leaving nothing out.

Breakfast, then school, then yoga,
Maybe a shower
Music, track, and homework
Dinner and soccer

Groceries and library,
Then clean the bathroom
Dishes, counters, laundry,
Sweep, mop, and vacuum

The thought of all I listed
Triggered intense stress
Maybe staying in bed
Might really be best

I fell onto the pillow
A groan escaped
Pattering feet entered,
"Mommy, time to wake."

Super Girl

Superman is in my bed
so, I climb in next to him.
He wraps his arms around me
and I hide from the world,
because tonight I don't want to be Super,
tonight I don't want to be Incredible,
tonight I just want to sleep,
and let the world go on without me.

Have I Done Enough?

I have always been confident
In the way I parent you.
Sure, I struggle and cry
But most days are smooth.

At home for 5 years
Seemed like forever to go,
Now I'm sitting here wondering
And I just need to know...

Have I done enough?
Have I taught you right from wrong?
Have I taught you when you're scared
That you can just sing a song?

Have I taught you to be a leader?
To answer questions, and be polite?
Raise your hand? Wait your turn?
To be kind with all your might?

Have I taught you to be smart?
To follow rules and obey?
To listen to your leaders
And follow what they say?

*****

Can you be nice to everyone?
Sit with those who need a friend?
If someone is being mean
You bring it to an end?

Today its just kindergarten,
Tomorrow junior high
Then high school and college,
It's all going too fast, I'm not going to lie.

Have I taught you that I love you?
That you are my stars, moon, and sun?
I love your mind, heart, laugh, and eyes
I love you, little one!

A Mother's Lullaby

Read a book
Sing a song
Close your eyes
And hum along
A kiss goodnight
And then another
I love you
Forever

Can I freeze time
And keep you just how you are?
Can I listen to your laugh
And hold you when you cry?
I want to always remember your eyes
And your smile
And your sunshine
You are the most beautiful girl,
Dear Angel,
Can I freeze this moment in time?

Tomorrow we start school
Together you and me
We'll learn to sit and follow rules
Learn to count 1, 2, 3

We'll learn our colors and letters
And learn some songs
Every day we will get better
Every day we will get along.

I'm excited to read books
And snuggle next to you
I'm excited to try cooking
I'm excited for all we'll do.

I love you, Son
To the moon and stars and sun
All the way there, all the way back,
I love you more each day, every single one!

My little angel
Guard of my heart
Stay with me always
Never to part

Lie on my shoulder
And kiss my cheek
Sweetest little girl
Gentle and meek

I'll give the world
Over to you
You own my entire heart
It's all for you

What more can I say
My little one
I am completely
Hopelessly won

I love you today
Tomorrow too
Always forever
I will love you

To the Man who marries my daughter:
Just remember, she will always be my baby
I held her the day she was born
I snuggled her to sleep
I sang hundreds, thousands of songs,
And read just as many books.
I kissed her when she fell.
I washed her dirty face.
I rocked away her fears
I melted from the look of her curious grey blue eyes
Or the half smile she gave when she was almost asleep
and she knew I was watching.
I can still hear her 2yr old voice call me mommy
I can still see her run with her pigtails bouncing along
She is my angel, my doll, my baby, my sunshine, my
laughter, my princess.
You may have her from Now until forever,
But always remember that I had her first.
You aren't Just marrying the Love of your Life,
You are marrying my daughter.
Her hand wrapped around my thumb when she was
scared
Her eyes lit up when I understood what she tried to say
I watched her play
I rubbed her cheeks and brushed hair from her eyes
I let her run around like a hippie with hair stringing in
every direction

*****

I dressed her up and braided her hair like the princess she is.
I tried to sleep as she lay next to me with her head on my shoulder and her hand holding mine
I pushed her on swings
I calmed her when strangers drew near.
She is one of the most precious things I have in my life.
She owns my heart.
Remember, on days when she gets stubborn, that I loved her first.

Cherubic Delight

Oh little Cherub
        How can you be so mischievous?
            The glint in your eyes
        Tells me you know just what you are
        doing
Then you smile like the angel you are
I can never stay angry with you
        You charm me with your laugh
Heaven must miss your seraph face.
        Through your playfulness
You bring peace into my life.

A Poem for my Baby

Your little hand holds mine
And I sing you a song
You smile up at me
And hum along

We rock back and forth
Eyelids are heavy
We both fall asleep
You against me

I Am Mom

Three people call me Mom,
ask me to read and sing a song.
I go places and they tag along.
Three people call me Mom

Three people hate me,
because I said they need to clean.
They have to pick up until nothing is seen.
Three people hate me

Three people love me today.
We run outside, blow bubbles and play.
You're the best, I hear them say.
Three people love me today

Three people call me Mom.
Some days are quick and some are long,
but I wouldn't trade them to anyone.
Three people call me Mom

"The song of the Angel"

Sleep, precious child
I am with you tonight.
No harm will befall
No fear at all
I am with you tonight.
Sleep, precious child

Sleep, precious child
As I hold you dear
Sweet kisses I bring
Sweet songs will I sing
As I hold you dear
Sleep, precious child.

Sleep, precious child
I love you so
I watch from above
From heaven with love
I love you so
Sleep, precious child.

In honor of Holly Bartlett Cowles
(1955-1987)

Father in Heaven

Dear father
In heaven above
Help me to care
And show lots of love

Help me to be
Your hand and your arms
Help me bestow
Your heavenly charms.

Help me to care
For your little ones
And to remind them
Of their home above.

A Goodnight Kiss

Remember that time
I gave you a kiss
I held you so tight
Just like this?

Remember I said
That you could fly
I lifted you up
To touch the sky

Then I tucked you in
And said goodnight
I left you to dream
All through the night.

What do you see
When the moon shines down
And spills her moonlight
All over the ground?

What do you feel
When it's late at night
With the moon on your face
And you're tucked in tight?

What do you hear
When the train comes or goes
Do you feel the rumble
Or hear the horn blow?

Do you know that angels
Come to be near
To kiss you goodnight
And hold you dear?   *****

What do you dream
When it's late at night
When you are fast asleep
With your eyes shut tight?

Do you dream of hope
And happiness and love?
Do you dream of the angels
And heaven above?

But what of the times
When you whimper with fright?
What do you dream
On those dark nights?

Of villains or dragons
Flying up in the air?
Or witches or wizards
Casting spells everywhere?

I wish I could be there
To wake you up
Tell you I love you,
My little Love.

I hope and I pray
As I tuck you in bed
And you start to drift off
And dreams enter your head

That they are the types
Which aim to inspire
Teach that you come
From some place higher

*****

98

That when you wake up
You are peacefully happy,
Ready to go
And ready to be.

I know that your night
Is full of dreams
Imagination runs rampant,
Or so it seems.

It's the time of day
Where you can be anything
A doctor or athlete
A Princess or King.

So I'll leave you to dream
I'll say sleep tight
I'll give you a kiss
And wish you Good Night.

What I wish I could tell the Me with one child:
Be happier
Relax; it doesn't get easier
Clean, because you can
Take time to sit and play
Do nothing
Listen to him laugh
Watch him grow
Make dinner while there aren't 50 different opinions
about food
A load of laundry a day keeps the piles away
Make your bed, you'll feel better
Grocery shopping is SO easy with one child compared to
three.
Take advantage.
Enjoy the moment.

A Song

You were born with a song,
A melody inside,
A breath full of notes
Unwilling to hide.

In the beat of your step,
In the glide of your run,
The rhythm of words
Consistently sung.

Harmony follows and
Leaves a song in your wake.
It's all around you,
The music you make.

Acknowledgements

Thank you to my family for being the muses by which I write. With out them, my life would be boring and dull. Thank you to my Mom for always encouraging me to write and for watching my kids while I do. A big THANK YOU to my Nana who wanted to see my name in print and put this book idea into my mind. Thank you to Tiana for the beautiful cover. She caught my vision so well. And to Catherine for being my sounding board when it comes to writing. Lastly, thank you to KC, my muse for all things Prince Charming. I love you.

About the Author

Brookie Cowles is a novelist at heart, but when poems pop into her mind, she writes them down. Most of her inspiration comes from caring for her three children and from ten years of marriage. She lives in beautiful Utah and loves the Fall season best. You can often find her reading a book, listening to a book, or writing a book. Her proudest accomplishment is passing that love of books to her children. You can see more of what Brookie does on her website www.brookiecowles.com

www.ingramcontent.com/pod-product-compliance
Lightning Source LLC
Chambersburg PA
CBHW020552030426
42337CB00013B/1069